Jesus and I

Anna L. Harley-James

ISBN 978-1-64492-800-4 (paperback)
ISBN 978-1-64492-801-1 (digital)

Christian Faith Publishing, Inc.
832 Park Avenue
Meadville, PA 16335
www.christianfaithpublishing.com

Printed in the United States of America

This book is dedicated to those who have made this journey over the years with me.

First and foremost, to Father God in the name of Jesus Christ our Lord. I never cease to worship and to give you praise, glory, and honor. Thank you for your divine presence. I trust you completely.

To my beloved children and godson, Cheryl Ann, Erick Kelvin and wife, Tawana Ann, belated Donald Fredrick, Audrey D. and husband, Carlos, Nicole Janell, Edward, Douglas and wife, La Tonya.

My precious sisters: Missionary Rosetta and husband, Deacon L. Hendry; Missionary Faye and husband, Deacon E. Saunders; Reverend V. Olivia and husband, Mr. J. Latty; Minister Mary Maddox; Ms. C. Davis and Ms. D. Harley; belated brother, Rudolph Henry Harley.

To my beloved belated husband Billy James.

One of my blessed spiritual daughters and sons, Sister Charlotte and Brother Leroy, Street Music of Ministry.

My devoted and caring pastor, Bishop A. L. Foxworth and loved wife, Elder K. Foxworth.

A godsent friend, Sister Earnestine Jones.

My loved prayer partners, Brother L. Burroughs, Missionary C. Sloan and husband, Deacon L. Sloan, Elder L. Bennett.

One of my precious spiritual daughters, Evangelist M. Silver.

One of my devoted spiritual sons, Pastor R. Harris and loved wife, Minister E. Harris.

One of my devoted spiritual sons, Deacon A. Watson and wife.

To physical therapists at Health and Sports Rehab, Inc.

To my two special ones Bernadette Fernandes and Timothy Szyp.

May all be blessed of God!

Jesus and I

Oh, when I think of the goodness of Jesus and all *he has done for me*. My soul cries out, "Glory! Hallelujah!" I thank God for his sovereign mercy and his grace.

My testimonies are to encourage, uplift, and inspire. God is a miracle-working God!

"Pronounced clinically dead."

December 1994, I was attacked with a cold virus. With all the home remedies used, it did not help. I sought medical help. With all the care given, nothing seemed to help. The virus was with me for a year. It wasn't getting better. The medical physicians did many tests. The last test that was done was a diagnostic testing for autoimmune disease: the result was there was an auto deficiency.

What happened when I didn't listen to God?

One summer, my family and I went to Georgia to spend time with my dad. During the visit, he gave me a large envelope and asked me to hold onto it for him. I said okay with a surprised expression, so he said, "You can read it if you like." When we arrived home, I put it away. Sometime later, the thought crossed my mind—you should look into what your father entrusted you with. I thought, okay. I opened the envelope and took out a long white form at the top was written, "What My Family Should Know." I said, "Wow." As I opened it up, I saw My Legal Will. I was impressed that my dad entrusted me with such an important document. I was amazed that out of seven children, he selected me, the middle child, to be second in charge of his will and testament. I called two of my siblings and told them Dad had given me his legal will to hold. Surprise, surprise, they were.

December 1995, on a Thursday evening, during our Bible study at home, a word came forth, "Anna, prepare yourself to go home." Home! My god, is it a spiritual death to be with you, or am I going to my birthplace Georgia? I knew I wasn't doing well in my body, but I was not ready to depart this life.

The first thing I did was pray for guidance, direction, and clarity. In a few days my children came in with a surprise for me. "Mother, we are getting you a ticket to go home." Thank you, Jesus.

Home is Savannah, Georgia. I began to praise God for clarity. I had an appointment with the doctor on Monday morning. After she finished her examination, she said, "I advise you not to go." I remembered what Proverbs 4:20 said, "My son, attend to my words, incline thine ear unto my sayings." Okay, God had already spoken; I must listen to him. (Man has facts; facts pull you away from the truth. But God has truth.) I made arrangements to go and spend time with my dad. When I arrived at my dad's house approximately 2:00 p.m., I found him in bed. Oh, no, not my dad this time of the day? Usually he is working in the field, around the house, in the yard, or working inside the house, but in the bed? No way.

I entered his bedroom and said, "Hi, Daddy."

He said, "Hey."

I asked him how he was and if there was something wrong. He didn't answer; he covered his head with the covers. By this response from him, I felt that he wanted to be left alone. So I decided to join my sisters in the kitchen. As I entered, they asked me if I was going to attend a family member's funeral. I said, "No, I did not come to attend a funeral. I came to spend time with Daddy."

I asked my oldest sister how long had Daddy been in bed. Her response was, "Daddy had not been in bed." This was something new. She said she prepared food for him daily and noticed that he was not eating. I'm not sure what my facial expression was, but she then said, "Anna, for real, Daddy was not down in bed." After the conversation, both of my sisters prepared themselves and soon left to attend the funeral. I then went into Dad's room and asked him to sit up on the side of the bed so he could eat something. I noticed that he was struggling to sit up. After he sat up and settled down, I washed his face and hands and applied lotion to add moisture. I then warmed a bowl of soup that my sister made earlier that day. I brought him a bowl and placed it on a tray next to his bed and asked him to try to eat. I stepped out of the room to give him privacy. I returned within a short time to check on him. He was trying to bring a spoonful of soup up to his mouth, and because he was shaking so badly, there was no soup left on the spoon. I said, "Let me help you, Daddy," and I fed him. Wow, I thought to myself, I wonder how long had he been like this and when the last time was that he had actually eaten.

After he finished the soup and drank a glass of juice, I wiped his hands and mouth, and he laid down to rest. I used that time for just me and Daddy. I was talking to God, trying to figure out what was going on and what was my purpose for being there. A few hours had passed before my sisters returned home from the funeral. When they arrived, I was in the kitchen tiding up. Daddy called me into the room and instructed me to get chairs and place them around his bed. He was very specific of what chair, how many chairs, where to get the chair, and where to place the chair.

While I was attending to his requests, my sisters were in the kitchen discussing the fact that Daddy could not be left alone. I entered the kitchen during the conversation only to discover that they had already made plans for him. I suggested that they should talk to Daddy about what they were planning to do for him so that he could have a say in the matter. It was then we heard him yell from his bedroom. We all got up and rushed into his room. Daddy told us to sit down. After we all sat down, there was one vacant chair left next to the head of his bed. My oldest sister asked him how he felt. He said with a hurt voice, "I don't understand. My sister has cancer, and she is doing well. I have cancer, and I don't have long to live." What! Cancer? We then found out as well that he was under hospice care; he was in the last stage. Wow, we didn't know. Daddy was diagnosed with prostate cancer, and he did not want his children to know.

After a moment of silence, my oldest sister asked, "Daddy, how do you feel spiritually? Is your soul well with the Lord?"

He answered, "I don't know."

So she turned, facing me, and said, "Anna will pray with you."

I said, "Daddy, our Heavenly Father will forgive you if you forgive those who sin against you. But, Daddy, if you refuse to forgive them, our Heavenly Father will not forgive you. Daddy, if you confess your sins to our Heavenly Father, you can depend on him to forgive you and to cleanse you from every wrong you have done because Christ died to wash away our sins." I began to intercede on behalf of my dad, and he took over the prayer. He poured his heart out to God asking for forgiveness.

He began to pray for his nieces and nephews and other family members. During the prayer, one of his nieces walked in and sat in the one vacant chair that was next to the head of his bed. She then began to pour her heart out to God. He ended the prayer with thanksgiving and praise. What a glorious time.

My father looked at me and said, "Anna, help my people." We thank God for answering the prayer of salvation. Later that night, I called my youngest sister and told her I needed her to come down to Georgia and stay with Daddy while I go back to Boston to get things situated and to bring my youngest son back with me to take care of Dad. She said okay. One of Dad's last requests was to walk around his house to view his garden and the house he built. Of course, at this stage of his illness, he was not able to walk. My sister rolled him outside in his wheelchair. He insisted on walking, so she helped him stand up, just as he took a few steps he collapsed.

We were able to help him up and back into the wheelchair. My sister then wheeled him around the back of the house. There he was able to look at his grape hopper and small field where so many collard greens, watermelon, and so much more were harvested. She then rolled him around the side of the house where a huge pecan tree stood and still stands to this day. And finally, to the front of the house where he labored every day the Lord sent in his flower bed. She finally rolled him inside, and we helped him back to bed. Dad was very weak; once he was settled he laid quietly. I can only imagine the thoughts that were going through his mind because I know what was going through my mind. I was not ready for my dad to leave, and I wanted so much to spend as much time with him that I could. So my plan, as I said earlier, was to go back to Boston, pack up my things along with my son, and return ASAP.

The very next day, my sister from Ohio walked through the front door. I left for Boston the following day to make preparations to come back. But before I could return less than a week's time, Daddy went home to be with our Lord. It all happen so quick, it was in the matter of days that he passed. After the death of my beloved sister, my mother, my husband, and now I had to prepare for the busy life of my beloved Daddy coming to a close on October 11, 1995. Preparing to go down for my dad's funeral service, my older sister called to remind me not to forget to bring the will.

When I arrived in Georgia, I wanted to give it to her, but she said, "No, you hold on to it." It was the way she said it. Well, I felt some kind of way. Her statement was the beginning of something (red flag), but I let it pass over. The evening of the funeral service, I was laying across my dad's bed, trying to process his death. It was so hard for me, I think, because of the quickness and how it happened. Him being sick and did not want his children to know—man, that was very hard for me to accept to this day. My caring children continuously checked on me to make sure I was okay. Everyone else seemed to be doing okay, fellowshipping as usual. I was having a problem dealing with and accepting that my dad was gone.

I remember saying when I saw him lying in the coffin that did not look like Daddy. My brother-in-law said, "Yes, Anna, that is him and he is gone." That saddened me the more, but I remained calm. As I type this, it brings back so many memories that I am in tears as I am typing this. Father God, please help me through this.

My youngest sister came into the room and said, "Anna, our sisters are waiting on you," which I was not aware of. I asked, "For what?"

She responded, "She is calling a meeting." I distinctively heard the voice of God say, "Don't move." She returned a second time and said, "They are waiting for you." I did not move. The third time, she returned and asked me if I was okay. Because I hold a special place in my heart for her, I did not want her to think there was something wrong with me. I got up and went in the kitchen to join them.

My oldest sister said the meeting was being held at my uncle's home. We were instructed not to bring any of our children. See, right there that was a red flag. I should have known something was not right. As we entered my uncle's home, everyone paired off except for me. I was standing alone, Jesus and I. It was then she asked her husband to open the meeting with a prayer. After the prayer, she asked me to read the will. Red flag. I heard to said no, so I said *no*!

She then called another sibling to read the will. It seemed as though she was very glad to read it. Oh my goodness, when she read the part that Daddy said, Anna was second in charge. It was all over for real. It was like a nightmare; all hell broke loose. It was a traumatic time for me. Oh, Jesus, my Lord. If you could imagine the worst, the worst it was. I can't think of anything worse that could have happened to me at that time. I was verbally attacked and accused of persuading my dad to make me second in charge. I can't image anyone persuading my dad to do anything. Why would I want to be second in charge? If you knew my dad, you would know that what I was being accused of was definitely not the truth. They refused to hear anything I had to say; in fact, my brother and brother-in-law from New York spoke up in my defense.

I cannot tell you how broken I was. First, my body was attacked with a cold virus that I was still dealing with; second, my dad died which was heart breaking; and now *all* my siblings accused me of something that was not the truth. God, *help*!

Needless to say, the trip was cut short. I returned to my dad's house alone, said to my children, "Let's go now!" We gathered our things and left for the airport. This should have been a time when a family pulls together during this time of loss, but instead it was a time of abandonment, hurt, and disappointment. I had fallen into a state of mental anguish.

My Overcoming the Feelings of Rejection, Brokenness, and Hurt Relationship with My Sisters

"A spirit of jealousy entered in."

My parents had ten children; one passed shortly after her birth.

We were raised as a very close-knit family with the fear of God in our heart.

After arriving back to Boston after the episode. That was the most humiliating experience I ever went through. My thoughts and anxieties had gradually increased. I went to my room and fell upon my face before the Lord. My cry was, "Lord, how can I be healed from such rejection, hurt, and broken relationship among my sisters?" The hurt was so great, it prevented me from functioning properly.

The most common cure I know is time. I didn't expect it to happen overnight. It took much time of praying for God's guidance and reading and meditation on the Word of God. I know healing can never come from our own efforts but only from the *Lord*. From all the hurt, I began to get very angry first; I felt like it should have never happened. I was accused of something that was not the truth. Second, I didn't have a chance to mourn with my sisters due to what had happened. I felt forced to leave earlier than planned. Lastly, I was not given the opportunity to visit my dad's grave before my return home.

Making God's Word Personal to Me

Oh my, when God's word came forth, "Anna, prepare yourself to go home," this experience has truly taught me some things. One major lesson I learned was believing and knowing that God will never lead us or direct us contrary to what he has taught or promised in his word. (Titus l:2)

> My sheep hear my voice, and I
> know them, and they follow me.
> (John 10:27)

Those who hear God's voice are those who belong to him. His sheep will hear and recognize his voice. We will hear his voice when we spend time in prayer and studying his Word. When you are asked to pray, what a great privilege—what a difference your prayer can make in the life of a dying person.

You not knowing that will be the very last prayer that person will hear! Father, oh, how I love you.

Prayer is very powerful, and prayer is not a duty, but it is a privilege. When I look back, oh my god, if it had not been for the Lord on my side, I within myself could have said, "You are the oldest, why don't you pray!" I just could not understand why she said, "Daddy, Anna will pray with you," out of everybody else in the room, including herself. But, Father, I am so very grateful and thankful to God that you, Father God, caused me to be obedient at that precious time of my dad's life. But, my Father God, I give you the highest praise that you truly was in charge. Thank you. My praises are for you alone. I declare this was truly a lesson learned for me.

Yes, it was. I learned, first, to consider the source when I don't understand what God is doing in my life. "I am Alpha and Omega, the beginning and the end, the first and the last." (Rev. 22:13) God is omniscient. God is almighty and all-powerful; but even so, he cares for each of us personally.

Second, to trust the Lord. "Trust in the Lord with all thou heart and lean not unto thine own understanding." (Prov. 3:5) From this, yes, I want to learn a new habit, saying, "I trust you, Jesus," in response to whatever happens to me. I now practice saying, "I trust you, Jesus," and this will help me to see him in every situation. My continual assertion of trusting God will strengthen our relationship and keep me close to him.

Third, to be obedient. "Obedience is better than sacrifice." (1 Sam. 15:22) Amen. "He that hath my commandments, and keepeth them, he it is that loveth me: and he that loveth me shall be loved of my Father, and I will love him, and will manifest myself to him." (John 14:21) Jesus said his followers show their love by obeying him. Love is more than lovely words; it is commitment and conduct. If you love Christ, then prove it by obeying what he says in his Word.

Lastly, to let God lead you. "Now the Lord had said unto Abram, 'Get thee out of thy country, and from thy kindred, and from thy father's house, unto a land that I will shew thee.'" (Gen. 12:1)

"It was by faith that Abraham obeyed when God called him to leave home and go to another land that God would give Him as his inheritance. Here it is, he went without knowing where he was going." (Heb. 11:8)

As much as we would like God to give us "what, where, when, and how," God just don't operate like that. Sometimes God will place us in a certain situation where we will have to trust him, and he will only give us a portion as we obey and trust him. We must remember and we must understand that faith is to trust God when we don't even understand God's plan for us. We must not be wise in our own eyes. We should always be willing to listen to and be corrected by God's Word and wise counselors. Bring your decisions to God in prayer, use the Bible as your guide, and then follow God's leading.

Not long after this earnest prayer on December 5, 1995, at approximately 7:00 p.m., God demonstrated his divine mercy, grace, and love for me.

My inner cry was, "Lord, my desire is to know you as my father and to obey you. Help me to have a true personal relationship with you, and I desire to see your divine glory demonstrated in my life. King Jesus, please fill me with your wisdom, direct my steps, and please make things clear to me."

However, I was not aware of the mysterious way that God would grant my request. After all, who knows the mind of God? "For who hath known the mind of the Lord, that he may instruct him? But we have the mind of Christ." (1 Cor. 2:16)

After praying that night, I said good night to Jesus, and I went to sleep.

Isolation

I wasn't sure of how the relationship was going to be fixed with my sisters. All I knew was I believed and trusted God to fix it. I knew it was nothing I could do, nor anything I wanted to do. There was no communication from me or my sisters. With my daily activities, my mind was always occupied with what happened, as much as I was trying to put it all out of my mind. I felt so alone and isolated from my sisters, and if I told the truth about it, I didn't want to have anything to do with them ever again in this life.

But I know according to the Word of God and my parents teaching, we are bound to be hurt and disappointed. When we live in a fallen world where good behavior is not always rewarded and bad behavior is not always punished, innocent people sometimes suffer. If God took suffering away whenever we asked him to, guess what? We would follow him for comfort and convenience, not out of love and devotion. Regardless to the reasons for our suffering, Jesus has the power to demonstrate his divine mercy, grace, and love in my life to help us deal with it.

Please hear this. From that, I learned this—when we suffer from whatever tragic events or reasons, please try not to ask, "Why did this happen to me?" or "What did I do wrong?" Instead, ask God to give you strength for the trial and offer you a clearer perspective on what is happening. Come on now, it's a learning process. But what we choose to do with that hurt, rejection, disappointment, being falsely accused can make us stronger in our walk with the Lord, knowing God promises to walk through the disappointments in life with us. Yes, God did say he will never leave me nor forsake me. His grace and his comfort are ours as we rest in him. Thank you, God. You have prepared each of us with unique opportunities to walk through all things in this life. So we can either walk in our own strength, which is our flesh, or we can walk in the power of the Holy Spirit. There you have it; it is our choice. My choice was to walk with the Holy Spirit, but I was not sure of how that was going to begin. In remembrance of the accident or incident on the night of Bible study, I was driving back from the store when the accident or incident occurred.

I said an accident; God said an incident.

The very next day, I was involved in a very serious truck accident. I was driving a Windstar van when I was hit by a speeding car. The car hit my front bumper on the right side of the truck so hard with such a violent impact, my van was turned completely around in the opposite direction and rolled down a hilly street. After I applied the brakes, it came to an instant stop. Then I applied the emergency brakes and attempted to get out of the van; however, the air-bag exploded, and the seatbelt tightened up around me. I struggled in my attempt to exit the vehicle. Just as I put my left leg out of the van to get out, the van began to roll down the hilly street and slammed into an oak tree with part of my body hanging out of the van. I was trapped between the tree and the van with the door closed on my body. I was pinned down; I could not move. I was squeezed so tight, I could not hardly breathe. I felt my breath being squeezed out of my body. I felt lifeless. I felt the spirit of fear taking over my spirit. I thought, "The spirit of life or the spirit of death, which one would it be?"

Instantly, I perceived God speaking in my spirit, "For I have not given you the spirit of fear, but of power, and of love, and of a sound mind." (2 Tim. 1:7)

I have learned that whenever there is faith, doubt will also come to challenge your faith. So we must always be ready to combat the doubt that will come against our faith. Immediately again, I perceived in my spirit, "For it is written, I shall give my angels charge over you, to keep you." (Luke 4:10) For it is written, he shall give his angels charge over thee, to keep thee. Oh, thank God, I begin praying, "My father, please send your angels to get me help." I felt lifeless as if I was going to pass out. I continued praying. I asked God to please sustain me until my help comes.

Shortly, I heard footsteps sounding like an army of soldiers coming to help me. When my help arrived, I was told to try to reach the steering wheel and put the gear in reverse. It was at this time I began to pray, "Father, please, have mercy and help me." It seemed like an extension was added on my arm, and I was able to reach the steering wheel and put it in reverse (I tried but could not do it before). I can't imagine what would have happen to me if I was able to have put the truck into reverse gear before when I first tried. Oh, thank you, my Father, for mercy, grace, and love. I gave my father the highest praise. Hallelujah!

The army of soldiers pushed the van away from the tree while a part of me was hanging out of the van. I fell out onto the ground. I was unconscious for a while. After regaining consciousness, I asked for someone to please call my children. A lady walked over and asked for their names and telephone number. I went unconscious again. When I regained consciousness, my loving daughter, Cheryl, and my loving son, Erick, had arrived. After arriving to the Brigham and Women's Hospital. I was rushed into the emergency room. Immediately, the attending doctor gave me the required care and attention I needed. There was broken glass in my hair. The doctor suspected that when I fell out the van, I must have fallen on some glass; however, there was no damage done. Again, I gave God the highest praise (Hallelujah!) after being examined and receiving the test results (which was good). I was released and put on bed rest.

After two weeks, my body began to display the following difficulties: problems lifting my arms, soreness when walking, limited movement in the joints, and aching muscles in my body. After three weeks of these symptoms, my primary doctor gave me a referral for physical therapy. After three months of treatment, three times a week, there had been no progress. I had become seriously ill. When I told her I was not getting better, she than wanted me to see a psychologist. I told her I know the problem was not in my mind, but it was in my body. I perceived in my spirit from the Lord to write out scriptures for healing. The Bible promises of God. Ones I could hold on to during this time of this acute illness.

> Surely he hath borne our griefs, and carried our sorrows: yet we did esteem him stricken, smitten of God, and afflicted.
>
> But he was wounded for our transgressions, he was bruised for our iniquities: the chastisement of our peace was upon him; and with his stripes we were healed. (Isaiah 53:4–5)
>
> Who his own self bare our sins in his own body on the tree that we, being dead to sins, should live unto righteousness: by whose stripes ye were healed. (1 Peter 2:24)
>
> That it might be fulfilled which was spoken by Esaias the prophet, saying, himself took our infir-

mities, and bare our sicknesses. (Matthew 8:17)

I am the Lord who heals you. (Exodus 15:26)

Therefore I say unto you, what things so ever ye desire, when ye pray, believe that ye receive them, and ye shall have them. (Mark 11:24)

And all things, whatsoever ye shall ask in prayer, believing, ye shall receive. (Matthew 21:22)

He sent his word, and healed them, and delivered them from their destructions. (Psalm 107:20)

He forgives all my sins and heals all my diseases. (Psalm 103:3)

I shall not die, but live, and declare the works of the Lord. (Psalm 118:17)

"I will give you back your health
and heal your wounds," says the
Lord. (Jeremiah 30:17)

My loving children posted them all around my
bedroom and wrote scriptures on my Kleenex tissue
boxes and placed them on my bed and nightstand.
They placed a tablet and pen on my bed beside me.

I confessed the scriptures out loud so that I
could hear them daily as many times as God spoke
them in my spirit. It is only when God's words get in
the midst of the heart and keeping God's word in our
spirit only then will the word produce healing.

So than faith cometh by hearing
and hearing the word of God.
(Romans 10:17)

Let them not depart from thine
eyes; keep them in the midst of
thine heart. (Proverbs 4:21)

So shall my word be that goeth
forth out of my mouth: it shall
not return unto to me void, but
it shall accomplish that which I

> please, and it shall prosper in the
> thing where to I sent it. (Isaiah
> 55:11)

God said, he sent his word and healed them or me and delivered them from their destructions.

> For they are life unto those that
> find them, and health to all their
> flesh. (Proverbs 4:22)

As long as I could see God's word, I read and confessed his word aloud so I could hear his words in my own ears and before my eyesight went dim. When my sight went dim then, I confessed God's Word from hearing the word being spoken in my spirit and from my memory.

When my son Erick Kelvin came up and saw me, he said, "Ma, you have to get out of this bed."

"Oh, no," he said, "this is not going to happen." To him that was the worst thing that could have happen. He was not used to seeing me in bed. What a time he had dealing with that. He would come at night and sit with me. Every time he came, I heard the same words over and over, "Ma, you have to get up and out of this bed." No doubt, he sat in silent prayer. When he thought I was asleep, he called himself tipping out, but I knew every time he left. I was not asleep. Bless his heart.

But as sickness began to take over my body, every time he came up stairs he would say, "Cheryl, come on, let's pray for Ma." Here comes my Cheryl with the bottle of oil anointing me from head down. She and Kelvin would get down on their knees around my bed and pray. My God, what a time that was. I remember Kelvin coming up, and Cheryl crying, telling him, "I can't get Ma to eat anything." Food was far from my mind. My organs began to shut down and swelling took place in my body from my stomach down. In the early '90s, this Evangelist and his wife came to our church. They would always have healing services. I would record all their services. What a glorious time of worship and lifting praises to God. The Holy Spirit would truly flow and souls would be saved and filled with the Holy Spirit.

> But the hour cometh, and now is when the true worshippers shall worship the Father in spirit and in truth. For the father seeketh such to worship him.
>
> God is a spirit: and they that worship him must worship him

in spirit and in truth. Worship comes from a different place within our spirit. (John 4:23–24)

Worship should be reserved for GOD alone.

It is through true worship that we invite the Holy Spirit to speak to us, convict us and comfort us.

Worship is intertwined with us surrendering to GOD: Be open to surrender, deny yourself take up his cross, follow him. (Matthew 16:24–25)

The people whom I formed for myself that they might declare my praise. (Isaiah 43:21)

I tell you that, if these should hold their peace, the stones would immediately cry out. (Luke 19:4)

Praise can be a part of our worship, but *worship* goes far beyond *praise*.

Praise is closely intertwined with thanksgiving as we offer back to God our appreciation.

This Evangelist husband and wife was given permission to run a revival of worship and praise. This is what we truly need today. These were anointed people of God.

On Friday nights, we had all-night prayer service. It wasn't nothing like worshiping until a word of God would be birth forth out of the Spirit of God. As worship came forth, the worship reflects John 4:23. Jesus said, "But the hour cometh, and now is, when the true worshippers shall worship the Father in spirit and in truth." The Holy Spirit overflowed, and everyone would cry out to God on one accord. Oh, what wonderful times of worship and praise that was.

While listening, feeling the anointing of the Holy Spirit, there was spiritual peace, joy, and rest. On the inside, a restoration in my soul took placed. Peace reigns continually. The emptiness I felt within was filled. My praising protected me from feeling self- pity. When you are occupied with praising and giving thanks, it is impossible to feel sorry for oneself. Worship, stillness, rest in God's presence, praises, and thanksgiving allows me to see the abundance God shower upon me daily. "In everything we must give

God thanks, for this is the will of God in Christ Jesus concerning you." (1 Thess. 5:18)

I perceived in my spirit to just relax and enjoy this journey in God's presence, trusting God to open up the way before me.

Praise and thanksgiving is richly seasoned with worship. "Oh, how we gave thanks to the Lord for he is good! For his mercy endures forever." (Ps. 118:28–29) Knowing that, just listen to how healing flows through worship and praise. Oh, how my very soul loves God.

Unexpected Visit

One of my sisters came to Boston on a business trip. She made a call to my son, asking him if it was okay for her to come over to visit me (before this visit, I had not heard from any of my sisters). He said yes. He picked her up from the hotel. When she walked into my bedroom, I could tell she was surprised to see the condition I was in. She said, "Hi, Anna."

I responded back to her. "Hi." She sat silent for a while. I am not sure what was going through her mind. As I said before, I was very surprised to see her. I was in and out of sleep for most of the visit. I am not sure how long it was before she broke the silence. She asked me how I was doing.

She then asked, "Anna, what happened?" Because of my nonresponse, she then said, "I don't know, it was a smoke screen, it should not have happen." She began to weep and said, "I am so very sorry." I responded, "Yes, I am sorry too." She didn't say much and didn't stay very long. When she was ready to leave, my son drove her back to the hotel after a few hours. During the drive, she requested that he keep her informed of my condition. His response was, "No, if you want to know how my mother is doing, you call her." This was the beginning of the open line for communication. This swayed into the remaining of my sisters communicating with me.

I choose to claim the heritage of a child of God and move forward in grace, learning from the promises of God forgiveness of others and of oneself is a gift that you can give only because it is the gift that was given to me and you by our Lord Jesus Christ.

> Be ye kind one to another, tender-hearted, forgiving one another, even as God for Christ's sake hath forgiven you. (Ephesians 4:32)

This is Christ's law of forgiveness as taught in the gospels (Matthew 6:14–15; 18:35; Mark 11:26).

We see it in the Lord's Prayer: "Forgive us our debts, as we forgive our debtors." God does not forgive us because we forgive others, but out of his great mercy. As we come to understand his mercy, we will want to be like him. Having received forgiveness, we will pass it on to others. "Those who are unwilling to forgive have not become one with Christ, who was willing to forgive even those who crucified him." (Luke 23:34)

This has brought me and my sisters closer together than we have ever been. We even have conference calls just to keep in touch with each other. One of my mother's teachings was:

> Follow peace with all men, and
> holiness, without which no man
> shall see the Lord. (Hebrew 12:14)

This was warning against refusing to listen; if you listened, you will obey. Mother taught us that sin always blocks our vision of God, so if we want to see God, we must remove it from our lives. Holiness is coupled with living in peace. She always said we must pursue peace in order to become more like Christ.

My mother's motto as family: "My dear children, please make every effort to live in peace with one another."

Making God's Word personal to me changed my life.

A year later, my illness got worse. I had to make God word very personal to me. God's Word will not change your life until we let it become personal.

I only put my name in the place of pronouns or nouns in the scripture.

> Surely goodness and mercy shall follow Anna all the days of Anna life. And Anna will dwell in the house of the Lord forever. (Psalm 23:6)
>
> Anna shall not die, but shall live and declare the works of the Lord. (Psalm 118:17)

This is what I did to strengthen my faith in the Lord and to encourage myself. To me this was like God was directly talking to me.

And building my *faith* by confessing speaking and meditation of God's Word over and over.

> If Anna abide in God and your words abide in Anna, Anna shall ask what Anna will, and it shall be done unto Anna. (John 15:7)

Our trust in Jesus begins an everlasting personal relationship with God.

God's Word is his medicine. Directions for taking God's medicine is in Proverbs. 4:20–21. The key for my healing.

> My son, attend to my words; incline thine ear unto my sayings.
>
> Let them not depart from thine eyes; keep them in the midst of thine heart.
>
> For they are life unto those that find them, and health to all their flesh.

Devine Revelation

Pay close attention to what you hear. The closer you listen, the more understanding you will be given, and you will receive even more understanding. Those who listen to God's word the more understanding you will be given. But for those who are not listening, even the little understanding you have will be taken away from you.

I could hardly feel life in my body. I had severe weakness in my muscles throughout my body, in my neck, shoulders, arms, and legs. I experienced weakness in lifting, pulling, squeezing, and pushing. In my neck, shoulders, and lower back, I was experiencing a lot of twisting, pulling, and tightening of the muscles along with a twisting pelvic.

My fingers sometimes became numb and very tight. In addition, I experienced a hot, itchy, burning sensation in and on my face, in my head, and all over my scalp, as well as throughout my entire body. It sometimes felt like something was crawling over my body. My face in my ears, neck, chest area, stomach, fingers, and thighs all turned very dark.

It seems to happen during the times that the heat in my body would rise. An irritating sensation of itching and burning inside and outside of my body would often occur. My back would itch so bad, my caring daughter would get a soft brush and stroke up and down my back (my Lord, what a time that was). It can be described as if there were parasites crawling inside my body and on my skin.

I cried out, "Oh, my Lord, there are worms crawling inside of me." My caring daughter would say, "No, Mother, worms are not crawling in you." But I knew how I felt and what it felt like. Every day I would say, "Yes, Cheryl, worms are crawling inside of me."

She purchased a bottle of AIM Para 90, a parasites cleanser. After taking for ninety days, some of the itching subsided. They took me to a homeopathy doctor, and he connected me up to machine, and it printed out everything that was going on inside my body. The results were he could not understand why there was only one parasite in my large intestine (we knew why, because I took the Para 90). He said, "You was raised up eating pork, parasites associated with pork and pork products." So he put me on bulk fiber. When I return in one month, I was cleansed from all parasites. I praised God with the highest praise. Hallelujah!

Something I learned from my experience of parasites.

Everyone has parasites at one time or another. Parasites love life in the human colon because they thrive on human waste. So why not use common sense, wisdom, and clean up our colons regularly? One of the most effective ways to begin ridding yourself of parasites is with a detoxification of your entire body. Cleansing can help to remove parasites, mucus, and toxins that have built up in the colon.

Four steps to purging parasites:

1. Herbal colon cleansing.
2. Increase your fiber intake.
3. Reverse vitamin deficiency.
4. Know sources—prevent re-infestation.

After cleansing your colon, it's very important to restore certain bacteria to prevent unhealthy bacteria from inhabiting the area. Probiotics are the good bacteria your system needs in order to restore its healthy flora.

I was diagnosed with a muscle and skin biopsy called Chronic Overlap Syndrome.

Dermatitis: a connective tissue disease that is characterized by inflammatory disorder of the muscles and the skin.

Rheumatoid arthritis: a chronic progressive disease causing inflammation in the joints and resulting in painful deformity and immobility, especially in the fingers, wrist, feet, and ankles.

Raynaud's (ray-nods): characterized by spasm of arteries in the extremities, especially the fingers, brought on by constant cold; leads to severe pain and numbness.

Lupus: a chronic inflammatory autoimmune disease. The signs and symptoms tend to last longer than six weeks and often for many years. Something goes wrong with your immune system, which is the part of the body that fights off viruses, bacteria, and germs or "foreign invaders." The autoimmune system cannot tell the difference between these foreign invaders and your body's healthy tissues and organs.

"Auto" means "self" and creates auto-antibodies that attack and destroy healthy tissue. These auto-antibodies causes inflammation, pain, and damage to the body. Lupus can affect any part of the body, causing inflammation and damage to the joints, skin, kidneys, heart, lungs, blood vessels, and the brain. It is considered a rheumatic arthritis disease. Lupus is a disease of flares (the symptoms worsen and you feel ill) and goes into remission (the symptoms improve and you feel better). Lupus can range from mild to life-threatening. Lupus is not contagious. Scientists do not know what causes lupus.

Angelic Warrior Lupus Survivors Foundation states, "We are striving for a cure and a better quality of life for people affected by lupus and other autoimmune diseases. There is not a cure for lupus."

The rheumatoid arthritis specialist recommended that I take a medication called methotrexate. This medication can trigger a unique and dangerous form of lung disease at any time during your course of therapy. This reaction can occur at doses as low as 7.5 milligrams per week. (The anti-arthritis dose.)

Methotrexate possible side effects:

- Severe liver damage.
- Severe reduction in red and white blood cell and blood platelet counts.
- Severe diarrhea, stomach irritation and mouth or gum sore.

Death can result from intestinal perforation, loss of kidney function, nausea, vomiting, itching, rash, hair loss, dizziness, and increased susceptibility to infection. Unusual sensitivity to the sun. Acne, headache, drowsiness, blurred vision, respiratory infection, and breathing problems.

Loss of appetite, muscle aches, chest pain, coughing painful urination, eye discomfort, nose bleeds, fever, and infections, blood in the urine, sweating, ringing or buzzing in the ear. With even more side effects.

When I presented this information to the doctor, his reply was, "If you don't take this medication, don't come back." I said, "I trust you, God."

My concerned and caring son Erick said, "With all, those side effects, my mother is already experiencing some of those side effects without taking the medication. The side effect is capable of causing death! Doctor, would you give the medication to your mother?"

Oh my, if looks could kill, we would have been dead. His reply, "If she doesn't take it, don't come back."

I said, "In the meantime, you have me on a very high dose of corticosteroid, and I need to be tapered down off this medication."

He again replied, "Don't come back." I was taking the Prednisone 100mg three times a day.

At this time, my cry is "Lord, my body. Father, what is going on with my body?" I perceived God speaking in my spirit, "Because your body at this time contain a lot of chemicals and toxins, you will find your body slowing down. You must drink a lot of water. Your children must keep you drinking and eating." Thank you, God, for the barley green, beets, and the carrot juice.

A dry season, my cry is, "Father, please tell me what to do!"

Encouragement: "For I the Lord your God hold your right hand; I am the Lord; who says to you, "Fear not, I will help you!"" (Is. 41:13)

Once again, my Heavenly Father reminded me—remember the ways the body dispel: urinating, bowel movement, sweating, vomiting. You must remember, your body has a lot of chemicals and toxins. Your body must be rid of chemicals and toxic you must drink a lot of water. You must follow the pattern. Remember you take the Prednisone three times daily, remember to take the herbs three times daily. Get plenty of rest. Rest is the result of sleep. While sleeping, your body will shut down and healing will take place. Peace, rest, quiet, calm, and be still. Quietness and trust enhance your awareness of my presence with you. Come on to me and rest. Rest in my radiant presence. I am all around you, to bless and restore. Breathe me in with each breath. Amen.

Yes, it is time now for your physician to begin to cut back by bringing you down now off Prednisone. Amen.

But I gave all praises to my Father God. He instructed and directed me how to come down and off the Prednisone. Although this physician knew I was on a very high dose of Prednisone, he told me not to come back because I refuse to take another medication that was prescribed because it stated one of the side effect was it could cause a heart attack. Every week, I cut back one half dose until I was completely off. Thank you, Jesus. Won't he do it? Yes, he can and will do it and he did it for me. I give him the highest praise. Hallelujah!

God said, "*Trust me.*"

I love Sarah Young's devotions entitled, "Jesus Calling."

When you come before *me* with your prayer requests, place your concerns before *me*. Speak to *me* in an honest and straightforward way; pour your heart out to *me*. Then give *me* thanks for the answers that I have already set into action even before you can perceive results. When your requests come back to your mind again, just continue to give *me* thanks for the answers that are on the way. If you keep repeating your concerns to *me*, you will live in a spirit of unbelief. Give *me* thanks for how I am answering your prayers, and your mind-set will become more positive. Prayer of thanksgiving will keep your focus on my promises and in my presence.

> Be still, and know that I am God: I will be exalted among the heathen, I will be exalted in the earth. (Psalm 46:10)

> Continue in prayer, and watch in the same with thanksgiving. (Colossians 4:2)

> According to his divine power hath given unto us all things that pertain unto life and godliness, through the knowledge of him that hath called us to glory and virtue. Whereby are given unto us exceeding great and precious promises: that by these ye might be partakers of the divine nature, having escaped the corruption that is in the world through lust. (2 Peter 1: 3–4)

I perceived in my spirit another comforting assurance from my God: "And it shall come to pass that before you call, I will answer. And while you are yet speaking, I will hear." (Is. 65:24) Father God, I trust you.

When the flare up would come from the lupus, all I could do was cry and say, "Lord, I trust you." Whenever it happens, you can't even move. One time, I was attending my girlfriend's funeral service, I had a part in the service to do. I attempted to get up and a lupus flare hit me, I could not move.

My body swells up with inflammation and body temperature raises, all I could do was cry. It is unbelievable how much pain I was in. My pastor rushed over and asked what was the matter and he prayed for me. My children had to carry me out. I could not walk at all. You never know it's going to happen until it happens.

There is nothing you could do to get relief you just have to bear with it until it passes over. My Lord, what a time. What awful disease. Lot of food can cause it to flare up, so I had to take notice and try to remember what I ate just before the flare. So I had to change my ways of eating. My joints will get full of inflammation and heat. Putting ice will freeze the area; it will quiet down for a while until you start to hurt from the ice. When the flare comes, it lasts for four or five days to a week, and sometimes longer.

There are times you may go a very long time like a month or two without having any flares at all. The medication I was taking did not help the inflammation neither the pain nor the swelling at all. One time, I was on a very high dose of corticosteroid, and it did not help at all it kept me off balance.

One morning, I had just gotten out of the shower and was in the process of getting dressed. I left the bathroom and went into my bedroom to get something. On my way back into the bathroom, I lost my balance, fell onto the wall, and my foot hit the corner of the sink, and I broke my small toe. Now I had to make another trip to the hospital for my small toe. Oh, boy, the doctor wanted to put a rod in to hold my toe in place but I said no. He taped the small toe to the toe next to it until I could get to my podiatrist.

I made an appointment to see my podiatrist ASAP. He suggested that he remove the bone from the small toe. So now I have to have surgery on my small toe. I was bedridden for a few months until it was fully healed. At this point, I just stopped taking all medication. I searched for supplements and ate accordingly. I looked for my healing to come totally from God. I suffered for nineteen years with lupus.

During the flare ups, no sleep, no rest, naps in between. Father, I truly trust and love you very much.

September 3, 2015

Immune function and health deteriorates.

Sleep deprivation has the same effect on your immune system as physical stress or illness, which may help explain why lack of sleep is tied to an increased risk of numerous chronic diseases. I received another comforting assurance from my father:

I felt that nothing the medical field was doing was helping me. This was indicated from the quick deterioration of my body and the uncertainty of the doctors. During the time of numerous tests and medical referrals, I began to lose weight. I became very small, around ninety pounds. My body felt lifeless. My body stopped responding to all care. It continued to diminish and began to decline to a bent, downward sloped position.

At this point, deterioration and decay began to set in. This was indicated by the breakdown in my skin (sores on my arms and legs). The unpleasant order of my body was ill repute. The elasticity in my skin was gone, and every part of my body became droopy, especially in my arms and legs for instance. My muscle system executed grievous motion.

All the muscles within my entire body became disfigured, losing its firmness, and creating a hole-like formation within the muscles. It was during this time that it became impossible to sit, lay, stand, or walk without having excruciating pain, which caused both physical and mental anguish. There was severe weakness, muscle aches, tension, muscles tightness, and limited movement with inflammation in my face and running out the corners of my eyes. There was a reduction of vision and hearing. I had no taste or new growth of hair. I had lost all my hair.

My throat muscles were functioning poorly, making it extremely difficult to swallow. As a result, I had great difficulty drinking and eating for over six to seven months. For a period, I lost my voice. My body was on the way back to the dust. "All go to one place, the dust from which they came and to which they must return." (Eccl. 3:20)

My loving, caring daughter said, I was very quiet through the whole illness. She said I was a very good patient. There was a great amount of weakness in my hands, fingers, arms, hips, and thighs. I lost control of the muscles in my bladder and anus. My hemorrhoid were exposed.

The severe itching caused me to scratch, which left severe skin wounds. I did not feel life circulating in my body on any level. I could not stand or walk alone. I could not sit up. I had to be tied to the chair so I would not fall over. I could not clap my hands or even lift my arms for that matter.

I could not hold anything in my hands, arms, and fingers were numb the majority of the time. I could not do anything for myself; my daughter had to bathe and dress me. I experienced a rising of body temperature to an extreme degree.

My cuticles broke open with inflammation constantly running out. The dermatologist prescribed some medication for me to take and some ointment to put on my cuticles. However, after a month of taking medication and using the ointment, my condition got worse. The doctor said she had no idea on how to further treat my cuticles and the condition I was in. I thanked her for being honest with me and not allowing me to undergo any unnecessary experience. My body was filled with inflammation.

My primary doctor diagnosed me clinically dead.

Re: Anna L. James

To whom it may concern:

Patient is a fifty-three-year-old female with chronic dermatomyositis diagnosed by muscle biopsy. She has been steroid dependent for the control of her symptoms. Even on high dose of Corticosteroid, she has had only a partial response to treatment. Her most recent exam on November 11, 1997, revealed marked weakness.

Proximal upper extremity
strength 3+/5
Distal upper extremity strength
5-/5
Proximal lower extremity
strength 4+/5
Distal lower extremity strength
5/5

Her last CPK level was three thousand in September 1997. Given that her disease was initially diagnosed March 1996, I feel that Anna L. James is unlikely that she will not recover all her functions completely. She is disabled and needs much assistance from her family for her daily activities, daily living, including dressing, bathing, and food preparation.

Prednisone 200mg, four times daily from July 8, 1996–November 1997.

Sincerely,
Primary Doctor

During this time of being confined to the bed, I had time to reflect on all the people that I took care of and brought into my home to care for. In fact, as a little girl, my dad would send me down to the neighbors' house to do whatever they needed done. After being mistreated by others during my years of being a nursing assistant, I often wondered how I would be if one day I would become a patient. I worked in many hospitals, private homes, took private cases, convalescent home, nursing homes; I took care of babies, private cases as a sitter, caring for very ill or special need patients.

I took care of my son, Donald, who was diagnosed to live to be six years old because of his heart condition. He lived to thirty-six years, one month, and twenty-two days. He was born blind, some deformity in his feet, thirteen bleeding ulcers in his stomach, had a massive stroke, and had seven aneurysms in the brain, cerebral palsy, and scoliosis. I also took care of my mother who had a health condition, acute renal failure, end-stage renal disease, Alzheimer's, and dementia and diabetes. I also took in one of my sisters who needed acute care and had to be monitored around the clock. It was then revealed to me that my home was a "house of refuge."

Well, my precious, loving, and caring daughter, Cheryl Ann, told me I was very quiet, and I was very easy to care for. At times, I felt fear trying to grip my spirit. But God consoled me by inspiring my precious, caring daughter Cheryl Ann with words of divine inspiration: "Am I not who I am? Am I not God? Yes, I called you. Behold, I have graven thee upon the palms of my hands." She cupped her hands over me. "See, I have graven you upon the palms of my hands, I will never forsake or forget you. You are never out of my sight. I see, yes, I see. I know all about you my child."

Once again, my Savior consoled me. "Behold, I have graven thee upon the palms of my hands. Thy walls are continually before me." Yes, I thank you, Jesus.

Encapsulated God's Herbs and Prayers

My body continued to feel lifeless. I was at my wits end. However, one morning, I perceived in my spirit God speaking:

> "For I will restore health unto thee,
> and I will heal thee of thy wounds,"
> saith the Lord. (Jeremiah 30:17)

This is one of my favorite scriptures.

I *thank* God in remembrance and for the consolation through his word.

I thank God for my beloved children, Cheryl Ann, Erick Kelvin, and the late Donald Fredrick. I told them I don't want to be a burden on them, and I preferred them to put me in a nursing home. They said, "Mother, you don't know, you are already in a nursing home." Oh, what a blessing! I have the best caring and loving children in the whole world, and they continued to care for me. I give my Father God all praises.

My Deterioration Progressed

I was feeling lonely. I perceived God speaking in my spirit, "You don't have the time to be lonely. You are about to go home, if you do not declare my word of life over your life. Get my word in your sight, let my words not depart from your eyes. Get my word in your mouth. Get my word in your ear. Keep my word in your spirit. Get my word in your mouth, let my word infiltrate your spirit and become living life in you. My word must penetrate beyond loneliness, beyond your feelings, in your spirit through meditation, attending, muttering, ponder. Once my word penetrates, my word will surely bring health to all your flesh. My word is a healing agent. Inherent in my word is the capacity, the energy, the ability, the anointing, the power, and the nature to effect healing in your body regardless your situation. My word will produce healing of all kind. Speak my word. My word comes from the spiritual to the physical."

I had some very serious moments with my father, Jesus Christ.

I heard repeatedly, "Rest, sleep." I thought I was resting, I thought I was sleeping. One night, I experienced my spirit come up out of my body, facing my body. I was looking down on myself. I saw myself looking around my bedroom like I was anxiously looking for someone or looking at something. Then I perceived God speaking in my spirit saying, "No rest, no sleep, and no clairvoyance." My thoughts were turn to God in reflection and worship. Then sleep came. I began to dream about my deceased family and how much I missed them and wondering if I wanted to be with them. I felt myself drifting away into a deep sleep. I believe that I was on my way to meet my Maker.

Vision Experience: Dream or Night Vision

There is a difference between a dream and a night vision. A night vision requires little or no interpretation.

In addition to the actual vision seen, a night vision usually has a voice speaking that gives the primary meaning and message of the vision.

For example, in Acts 16:9–10.

> And a vision appeared to Paul in the night. There stood a man of Macedonia, and prayed to him, saying. Come over into Macedonia and help us. And after he had seen the vision, immediately we endeavored to go into Macedonia, assuredly gath-

ering that the Lord had called us
to preach the gospel unto them.

I fell into a deep sleep, and I was walking
through a long tunnel, not well lit. At the end of
the tunnel, there was a figure surrounded by bright
lights. As I was walking through the tunnel, I heard a
voice say, "Speak. I shall not die but live and declare
the works of the Lord." I was trying so hard to get to
the end of the tunnel, trying to walk fast but moving
very slow.

I was about halfway there when I heard the
voice a second time say, "Speak. I shall not die but
live and declare the works of the Lord." Finally I got
to the end of the tunnel. I was at the threshold, and
I heard for the third time, with the voice of thunder, say, "Speak. I shall not die but live and declare
the works of the Lord." I looked over, it was a very
quick moment, and good Lord Almighty, what did
I see? A city within a city, bands of angels, beauti-
ful music, melodious voices—it was impossible to
see God's face, but the Glory of God was shining all
around bright lights, different shapes of stones, gold,
silver, diamonds, pearls, and crystal stones cut into
precious gems. The voice of thunder bouncing back
and forth from one ear to the other. Then I heard,

"Speak, speak, speak, speak. You shall not die but live and declare the works of the Lord."

"Yes, Lord," I spoke, "I shall not die but live and declare the works of the Lord." I felt the presence of God quickly pulling me backward out of the tunnel. I was continuously saying, "I shall not die but live and declare the works of the Lord."

I then was awakened back to life. I was still speaking, "I shall not die but live and declare the works of the Lord." As long as I heard it in me, my spirit, I repeated it out loud.

My daughter, Cheryl Ann, ran into my bedroom with excitement. "Mother, what is the matter?" I was still speaking what I heard from my father, "I shall not die but live and declare the works of the Lord!"

God consoled me through my precious daughter Cheryl. "I sent my word and healed you," said the Lord.

"Yes. I trust you, Father."

I had to make God's word very personal to me knowing the Bible says that God sent his Word and healed them all.

I believed the key to me receiving my healing included the following—first, receiving healing for my mind and body, which is in God's Word; second,

I had to hear God's Word so faith will come into my heart; and lastly, I had to confess God's Word with my mouth before I could release my faith. I made my confessions out loud so I could hear God's word with my own ears three or more times a day, as often as God spoke within my spirit to speak.

I remembered Charles Capp's book entitled *The Tongue: A Creative Force.*

"Jesus said you can have what you say." (Mt. 21:22) The Word of God, in essence, said the tongue will cause the healing power to stop. It will set on fire the wheels of lineage, or that which you have inherited. What you have inherited is natural healing power in your body. Don't misunderstand, I am not talking about divine healing, but I am talking about the natural healing ability of the human body. I can cut my finger; I don't have to be concerned about it. My body knows how to heal itself. That healing power is in us.

If we talk sickness and disease and defeat, we have released words that will produce after their kind. We can stop the natural healing power that God put in our body by the words of our mouth. Many have stopped divine healing in the same way by negative words.

> Death and life are in the power
> of the tongue: and they that

love it shall eat the fruit thereof.
(Proverbs 18: 21)

Thou art snared with the words of thy mouth, thou art taken with the words of thy mouth.

The words we speak will either work to our good or work against us depending whether we are speaking Blessing or cursing. Speaking positively and in agreement with God's word. Speaking negatively or in opposition to God's word. (Proverbs 6:2)

For the word of God is quick, and powerful, and sharper than any two edged sword, piercing even to the dividing asunder of soul and spirit, and of the joints and marrow, and is a discerner of the thoughts and intents, of the heart.

Neither is there any creature that is not manifest in his sight: but all things are naked and

> opened unto the eyes of him with
> whom we have to do. (Hebrew 4:
> 12–13)

The Word of God is not merely a collection of words from God, a vehicle for communicating ideas; it is living, life-changing, and dynamic as it works in us with the incisiveness of a surgeon's knife. God's Word the core of our moral and spiritual life. It discerns what is within us, both good and evil. The demands of God's Word require decisions. We must not only listen to the Word; we must let it shape our life.

Words that we speak are the most powerful thing in the universe.

> Set a watch, O Lord, before my
> mouth; keep the door of my lips.
> (Psalm 141:3)

James wrote that "The tongue is a little member and boasteth great things. Behold, how great a matter a little fire kindleth!" (James 3:5)

On the average, a person opens his mouth approximately seven hundred times a day to speak. David wisely asked God to help him keep his mouth shut—sometimes even as he underwent persecution. Jesus himself was silent before his accusers (Matthew 26:63).

Knowing the power of the tongue, we would do well to ask God to guard what we say so that our words will bring honor to his name.

From this, my Father taught me this lesson.

God's Word is his medicine.

The key for our healing: Proverbs 4:20–21.

> My son, attend to my words; incline thine ear unto my sayings.
>
> Let them not depart from thine eyes: keep them in the midst of thine heart.

Pay attention to what I say, not what someone else say.

Listen carefully, incline your ear unto my sayings, hear what my word is saying, not what some else word is saying. Submit to what I say. Consent to my word, my sayings. Say only what I say. Let my words not depart from your eyes; keep my words in your sight, before your eyes. Don't let my words out of your sight. Keep my words in the midst of your heart. Keep my word in your spirit. It is only as

God's words get in the midst of your heart or spirit and stay there that the word produce healing in your body. We need God's words to infiltrate our spirit and become living or life in us! God's words must penetrate beyond our reasoning, all the way to and in our spirit, through meditation.

Approximately 2:30 a.m., I perceived in my spirit I was carrying my body around like a corpse for one year and six months, from January 1997 to July 1998. But God said, "As of this time, July 19, 1998, life and circulation has begun." Glory be to Jesus, my Father God. Oh, hallelujah!

My father led Reverend Graham a good praying friend of mine to call me. She knew nothing about me being in a car incident. She called to invite me to a service she was having. In the midst of the conversation, she asked if I knew anything about barley green. I said, I knew Jesus fed five thousand people with five loaves of barley bread and two fishes. She said, "Barley green is what you need."

Immediately, I perceived to ask her, "How can I get it?"

She said, "I will bring it to you." A few days later, she came over to bring me the barley green. She took one look at me, much surprised, she dropped the container of Barley green on my bed and left.

She didn't know that I had been in an accident, or as God said, an incident, and was as sick as I was. I was partially paralyzed on the left side of my body and could hardly use it.

I began to cry out to my father, "Father, I don't know what to do. Reverend Graham didn't tell me how to take this barley green." Early the next morning, the Lord woke me up, and I perceived in my spirit my father saying, "If you eat all uncooked food and take this barley green every hour. One tablespoon of barley green mixed in fresh juice every hour and every day for six months, your body will regain health."

So my precious daughter, Cheryl Ann, went to Whole Foods market and bought all organic fruits and vegetables. The number for organic, the number nine, for divine, that help us to remember the number nine for organic. She came home and began to juice celery, carrots, beets, parsley, apples, pears, spinach and kale, greens. That's just some of what she used. She didn't juice all of them at one time, just a good portion. Approximately about four ounces with a tablespoon of barley green every hour. My children spoon fed me this for six months.

We were told about a place by Reverend Graham named the Hallelujah Acres, which is located in

Shelby, North Carolina. My precious son, Erick Kelvin, called and asked what qualifications does one needed in order to attend. This place was originally for the medical people and their family. But now it is open to the public. They teach you how to eat for your healing. But recommended for us to buy was this book *God's Way to Ultimate Health*, a common sense guide for eliminating sickness through nutrition by Dr. George H. Brown with Michael Dye. This is one of the books they used in teaching how to eat for your healing. This can be bought from Barnes & Noble.

From this book, I was introduced to the barley green along with the Hallelujah Diet, which is an excellent way of eating for health. As I healed from the fresh juicing and the barley green, my daughter introduced me to the Hallelujah Diet.

What Is the Ideal Diet?

When God created man, he placed him in a garden setting and told him his diet was to consist of simply raw fruits and vegetables.

"And God said, 'Behold, I have given you every herb (vegetable) bearing seed, which is upon the face of all the earth, and every tree in which is the fruit of a tree yielding seed, to you it shall be for meat (food)" (Gen. 1: 29). How did man fair on such a diet? He lived an average of 912 years, without any recorded sickness. Following the flood in Genesis, meat was added and man started to cook his food. As a result of these two changes in the way man ate, the life span rapidly declined in ten generations from an average of 912 years to 100 years.

Today, we have moved even further from God's original diet by putting increasingly more toxic substances into our bodies, so that today, by the age of forty, the average person already has serious physical or health problems. The most important things needed for self-healing are fresh air, pure water, adequate rest, internal and external cleanliness, sunshine, a positive mental attitude, vigorous exercise, and eating the foods created by God for our nourishment. And the only nourishment God ever intended for us to put into our bodies is pure water, fresh air, sunlight, and fresh raw fruits and vegetables.

As long as these needs are met, the body is self-sufficient and will function properly in perfect health. But when we deviate from these basic biological needs, the human body becomes clogged and poisoned, energy is depleted, physical problems result, and life is shortened. If we would but return to God's ways of nourishing the body. We could practically eliminate sickness from the face of the earth, and man would die only of accidents or old age at about 120 years (Genesis 3). You see, when we cook our food, we destroy its nutritional value, and we force the organs of our body to work overtime to remove the toxic residue, which tires the body, produces illness, and shortens human life to only a fraction of what God intended.

> And the Lord said, "My spirit
> shall not always strive with man,

for that he also is flesh: yet his day shall be an hundred and twenty years." (Genesis 6:3)

What Is Barley Green?

By Dr. George Milkmus

Alive, naturally potent, organically grown food produced from the juice extracted from young barley leaves when they are ten to fourteen inches in height. But after the juice is released from the fiber, it becomes very fragile and unstable, subject to oxidative decomposition threatening the nutritional enzymes, vitamins and chlorophyll. To stabilize and preserve the juice, it is spray-dried onto a water-soluble, complex carbohydrate, in this case, Maltodextrin. Derived from corn, the malt dextrin replaces the role formerly held by the plant fiber and keeps the nutrients from oxidizing. The advantage is that malt dextrin dissolves in water, unlike plant fiber, allowing the nutrients to be absorbed directly into the bloodstream within minutes, without going through the digestive process. Dr. George Malkmus said, "Beware of any barley juice powder that does not contain maltodextrins"

Small amounts of powered brown rice and kelp are added to barley green. Brown rice is a rich source of Vitamins B-1, B-2, nicotinic acid, and linoleic acid, while kelp is a good source of trace minerals missing in the American diet. Barley green is alkaline in PH, an important antidote for our high acid-ash, high protein American diet. Unlike drugs or medications, barley green has no adverse side effects. One tablespoon of barley green contains approximately twenty-two calories. (The bright green color of barley green is the natural chlorophyll, with no artificial colors or flavorings added.)

What Nutrients Are Found in Barley Green?

Because barley green is a high quality, balanced, nature green food, it helps the body balance, cleanse, and heal itself. Consuming proper nutritional food builds healthy cells, allowing the body to maintain health and perform its natural healing powers

Vitamins and Minerals

Barley green contains at least sixteen vitamins, twenty-three minerals, and twenty enzymes. In fact, barley green is the most nutritionally dense food that has ever been found, providing one of the widest spectrums of naturally occurring nutrients available in a single source on the earth today! (Be sure to use the barley green with kelp.)

Enzymes

There is no function of the human body that does not require enzymes, or that does not suffer if their supply is insufficient. Enzymes are the catalyst for all chemical changes in our body, such as digestion of food, sending oxygen from the lungs to our blood and cells, body movement, synthesizing proteins from amino acids to make muscle, and even thinking. Barley green also contains the super scavenger super oxide dismutase (SOD), which destroys the damaging free radicals that lead to cancer, heart disease, and other illnesses.

Proteins

Barley green contains all the essential amino acids. It is 90 percent digestible protein and because its protein molecules are small, this protein will not stress the body as do protein molecules from meat.

Alkalinity

Barley green is alkaline, which helps neutralize the acidity from meat, starches, soft drinks, and preserved foods.

The Hallelujah Diet

Breakfast

One tablespoon of barley green powder, either dry or let it dissolve in my mouth or in a couple of ounces of distilled water at room temperature. If I get hungry before noon, I may eat a piece of fresh, juicy fruit late morning.

Cooked food was an absolute no-no as my body was in a cleansing mode until about noon each day.

Lunch

One tablespoon of barley green powder as at breakfast. Most of the time my caring daughter would stir my barley green with fresh carrot juice, about eight ounces. It is delicious and extremely nutritious. A raw fruit dish, she would switch from a fruit dish to a vegetable salad.

Supper

One tablespoon of barley green powder, either dry or in four ounces of distilled water or eight ounces of fresh carrot juice. Never canned, bottled, or frozen. At least thirty minutes after the barley green, a green salad (leaf lettuce, never head lettuce) broccoli, cauliflower, celery, carrots, some baked sweet potato, brown rice, steamed vegetable, whole-grain pasta, whole-grain bread, etc. A glass or two of organic apple juice or a juicy fruit. To be sure I get essential fatty acids needed by the body, put it on salad or take right from the bottle Barlean's High Lignan Organic Flax Oil.

This is not all the Hallelujah Diet. There is more. If interested, please get the book *God's Way to Ultimate Health*.

It Was Made Very Clear—
Restoration Time

Clearly, I began to recover. My beloved children, Cheryl and Erick, took me for short walks. My Lord, I could not walk well at all. I said, "Oh, my Lord, my children are losing their minds. I can't hardly walk. What is wrong with this picture? What is wrong with my children?"

But they took me for a walk at Franklin Park three times weekly. My son, Erick, diligently assisted me in doing strengthening exercises with assistance from my spiritual son, Andrew Watson. Andrew, my spiritual son, was continually persistent in treating me at is his business, Health and Sports Rehab, Inc. I was very blessed to have him as my spiritual son and my private physical therapist. I pray that God will keep him as the apple of the eye and hide him under the shadow of his wings forever. This helped a great deal with releasing much tension from my body.

Thanks be to God, from whom all blessings flow.

In God, I live. In God, I move. In God, I have my being.

> The voice speaking, gave the message of the vision, "I shall not die, but live, and declare the works of the Lord." (Psalms 118:17)

> For in death there is no remembrance of thee: in the grave who shall give thee thanks? (Psalms 6:5)

> What profit is there in my blood when I go down to the pit? Shall the dust praise thee? Shall it declare thy truth? (Psalms 30:9)

I declare I shall not die but live although God said I carried my body around like a dead body. But I decree and I declared that I shall not die but live in the precious name of Jesus.

God spoke as of July 19, 1998, approximately 2:30 a.m., life and circulation has begun saith the Lord.

At 3:00 a.m., I perceive in my spirit from the Lord, "You must highlight the beginning of life and circulation on July 19, 1998."

To God be the glory, honor, and the praise. Amen.

I can truly speak without a shadow of a doubt I perceive from God how I carried my body around like a corpus. A dead body for six months from January to July 19, 1996. But as of July 1998, life and circulation has begun. A warfare prayer covenant was made.

Healing herbal plants for:

- immune system
- treatment for inflammatory
- muscular skeletal system
- digestive system
- cardiovascular system
- complete body system.

Every morning, I wanted my daughter to get me up so that I could sit me upright in my chair. I didn't know why, and I would ask her to please open the venetian blinds, and she would say, "Mother, it is dark outside."

I would say, "But I want you to open the venetian blinds, please."

She would always say, "Why, Mother, it is dark outside." But I did not know why, I just want them opened.

One morning, after getting me up without saying a word, it was urgent for me to see outside. I looked like I was looking for someone or I was expecting someone or I was even looking like I was expecting to participate. I did not know why.

But this early morning, as I sat patiently, suddenly it was like I saw Jesus surrounded with many children. Oh, they were all in a circle, so many children. He was very busy attending to them, teaching, reading, feeding, loving, and caring for them. It seems like it was preparation time. I just watched him attending to the children.

So one morning, I asked, "Jesus, whose children are they?"

He said, "These are the children that were not wanted." But he was so busy attending to those children, he didn't look away from those children nor did he ever stop doing what he was doing. I was thinking about what he was preparing them for. I said, "Jesus, you are so busy." He was just moving real fast from one to another. It seems as though there was not much time, and he was getting done what he had to do before the end of the time. He looked around and said, "The Kingdom of God is at hand." Then my daughter walked in with my morning juice. The barley green, my friend.

One characteristic all children share is that they want to grow up, to be like the big children, or their parents. When we are born again, we become spiritual babies. If we are healthy, we will yearn to grow. How sad it is that they never grow up. The need for milk is a natural instinct for a baby, and it is necessary for growth. Once we see our need for God's Word and begin to find nourishment in Christ, our spiritual appetite will increase, and we will start to mature. How strong is your desire for God's Word?

> Jesus blesses little children. And they brought young children to him that he should touch them: and his disciple rebuke those that brought them. But when Jesus saw it, he was much displeased, and said unto them, suffer the little children

to come unto me, and forbid them not; for of such is the Kingdom of God. (Mark 10:13–14)

And Jesus called a little child unto him, and set him in the midst of them, and said, verily I say unto you, except ye be converted, and become as little children, ye shall not enter into the kingdom of heaven.

Whosoever therefore shall humble himself as this little child, the same is greatest in the kingdom of heaven.

And whoso shall receive one such little child in my name receiveth me.

But whoso shall offend one of these little ones which believe in me, it were better for him that a millstone were hanged about his neck, and that he were drowned in the depth of the sea. Amen. (Matthew 18:2–3)

D ecree and declare the promises of God.

> "For I will restore health unto
> you and I will heal you of
> your wounds," saith the Lord.
> (Jeremiah 30:17)

The medical language here conveys the idea that sin is terminal. It cannot be cured by being good or being religious. Beware of putting your confidence in useless cures while your sin spreads and causes you pain. God alone can cure the disease of sin, but you must be willing to let him do it.

> For all the promises of God in
> him are yea, and in him Amen,

unto the glory of God by us.
(2 Corinthians 1:20)

All of God's promises of what the Messiah would be like are fulfilled in Christ ("All the promises of God in him are yea.") Jesus was completely faithful in his ministry; he never sinned (1 Peter 3:18), he faithfully died for us (Hebrews 2:9), and now he faithfully intercedes for us (Romans 8:34).

I was introduced to Touch for Health Kinesiology, Iridology, and Herbal Program Development by Gene Fitzpatrick, CK, CI. Gene once was a quality control manager who believed firmly in conventional medicine but now practices holistic healthcare and uses herbs, muscle testing, and iridology. I know you might be asking, what is kinesiology?

It is a non-invasive method of evaluating and balancing the body developed by Dr. George Goodheart, DC, in the late 1950s that incorporates ancient Chinese arts of healing providing the benefits of acupuncture (without needles) and therapeutic massage (without taking your clothes off). Iridology is truly a proactive tool for health. Though modern iridology (the evaluation of the iris) has its roots in the early 1800s, this art and science dates back to ancient Egypt. By taking pictures of the irises through a forty power microscope, documents are provided that gives a full understanding of the current state of emotional and physical health as well as hereditary weakness. Muscle testing is a technique used to evaluate the body's imbalances and assess its needs.

September 3, 2015

I perceive in my spirit from the Lord to change doctors and change hospital.

I thank God I was obedient. My new primary doctor ordered blood work to be done. When he received the results, he said, looking at the blood work it looks like there is no lupus. So he said, I am going to send you for a second opinion, so he sent me to a rheumatoid arthritis specialist. She said that I am going to have some blood work done. When the results came back, she said there is no lupus and no rheumatoid arthritis in your blood and the chronic dermatomyositis levels are good. The level is down from three thousand to two hundred.

> O Lord, if you heal me, I will be
> truly healed; if you save me, I will
> be truly saved. My praises are for
> you alone. (Jeremiah 17:14)

Glory, hallelujah! I decree and I declare I am healed!

March 1996, I was diagnosed with lupus and rheumatoid arthritis. Nineteen years later, there is no sign of lupus and no sign of rheumatoid arthritis in my blood.

God said I am not a lupus survivor, I am healed from lupus. And dermatomyositis levels is down from three thousand to two hundred. Hallelujah!

Whose report shall I believe? I shall believe the report of the Lord. His report said I am healed. His report said victory. Doctors give facts but God gives the truth. I decree and I declare God has given me the victory. I am healed. I praise my God.

I am healed from lupus and rheumatoid arthritis. Praises to our God. Glory, hallelujah!

From this I have learned that we are designed to do a divine assignment.

If we want to know how to maintain wellness, we must first understand how we are made, how our body is designed to heal itself, and what food God created for our bodies to function properly. God said, "He is concerned about the whole man, body, spirit, and soul." For most of the two thousand years since Jesus established his church, Christianity has focused on the soul and spirit of man while ignoring the body, which is the temple of God. Yet my Bible says:

> What? Know ye not that your body is the temple of the Holy Ghost which is in you, which ye have of God, and ye are not your own?
>
> For ye are bought with a price, therefore glorify God in your body and in your spirit which is God's. Romans 12:1 I beseech you therefore, by the mercies of God, that ye present your bodies a living sacrifice, holy, acceptable unto God, which is your reasonable service. (1 Corinthians 6:19–20)

Psalm 139:14 says we are fearfully and wonderfully made. When God created man, he made us perfect. I believe with all my heart that God knew quite well what he was doing when he told us that he gave us plants for healing. Why do we try to change God's gifts? Let us just use them.

I remember Dr. Georgia H. Malkmus book entitled *God's Way*. And his glory will I not give to another.

Thanks be to God from all blessings flowing. Thank you for this the restoration state in my vulnerable time of wounds and physical injuries. Healing has taken place.

> God is not a man that he should lie; neither the son of man that he should repent: hath he said, and shall he not do it? Or hath he spoken, and shall he not make it good? (Numbers 23:19)

> "For I will restore health unto thee, and I will heal thee of thy wounds," saith the Lord. (Jeremiah 30:17)

Yes, this is one of my favorites.

Thank you, God, for this—the restoration state in my vulnerable time of wounds and physically being injured. *Healing* has taken place.

All praises, glory, and honor to Jesus my Lord and Father God.

Restoration is on the way. Yes! Thank you, Jesus!

I truly thank my father, Jesus Christ, in remembrance and for the consolation through his word. I thank my father Jesus Christ for my beloved caring children, Cheryl Ann, Erick Kelvin, and the late Donald Fredrick. I told my children I don't want to be a burden on them, I prefer them to put me in a nursing home. They said, "Mother, don't you know you are in a nursing home?"

My body begin to swell as my liver and kidneys were shutting down. My son, Erick, would come and say, "Cheryl, get the oil and let's pray for Ma." My daughter, Cheryl Ann, would rub me down with oil and they would pray. Father, I thank you. You have loaned me such blessed children. They truly are a wonderful blessing to me, and I truly thank you again and again. I have the best children in this world, and they continue to care for me.

This is the power of prayer.

One powerful way to pray is to find a scripture in God's Word and remind God what he said about you.

> Put me in remembrance let us plead together: declare thou, that thou mayest be justified. (Isaiah 43:26)

We must pray God's promises instead of our problems and then our attitude will change from victim to victor. God's Word coming out of our mouth will be powerful, decreeing and declaring the promises of God. I truly believe he will dispatch his angles with the answers. He sets miracle into motion, and he will begin to change things.

It may not happen overnight, but stay in faith and keep reminding God what he promised us day in and day out. Just don't complain. You just speak. God gave us the authority to speak to the situation. We must use our authority.

Don't beg God, just speak. "God, you said…" Don't describe the situation or the condition, just speak, "God, you said…" We must get in a habit practicing praying the promises of God. Put God in remembrance of his Word. God's Word and all his promises are *yes* and *amen*.

Update Report

M y cry was, "Lord, why can't I lift my head up off my pillow?" If I could lift my head up, I would be able to get up out of my bed by myself. Clearly, I perceived from God that a neck support would strengthen your whole body. My daughter preserved to get a soft cervical collar. God's efficient power directed me through getting up and out of bed by myself. No more ringing a bell for assistance with getting up. My whole body has become more stable, no more walking into walls, no more falling over head first when bending over. Now I am able to pick things up from the floor. Glory to God, I am able to stabilize myself when walking.

My vision is strengthened.

More control and stronger muscles in my face, my jaw bone strengthened. I am able to open my mouth. I am able to smile. My breathing is stronger and easier. For six months, I was not able to eat. My ability to swallow was extremely difficult. I can now swallow and eat better. I am also able to eat a variety of foods. The strength in my arms has returned as well as decreased tension. My blood circulation has improved, subsiding of pin sticks in fingers. Now I have better circulation in my arms and fingers. All my natural color has returned in my skin and fingers. Decrease of tension in the hips, and hips are feeling stronger. Muscles are starting to feel more relaxed and tension is decreasing. I am able to lift my legs in bed. I am also more stable when walking. Shoulders have subsided in slipping out of place. Bladder muscles are stronger, and I now have control over my urine. Anus muscles are strengthened and hemorrhoids have subsided. My smell and taste of food has restored. Overall, the toxins that caused the undesirable odor of the breath and the body has completely subsided. My posture has also improved. I am able to stand up right much better. My nerves are settled. I am now able to sit and lay down for longer periods of time. My overall reflexes are strengthened. Hallelujah, I will be courageous, I will be brave in Christ. To God be the glory and majesty, dominion, and power both now and forever. Amen.

Things Jesus and I can physically do:

- Jesus and I can get up out of bed.
- Jesus and I can turn my head from side to side without pain.
- Jesus and I can balance my body and am able to walk inside the house without falling.
- Jesus and I can step up into the van without the use of a step stool.
- Jesus and I can step down and up in the door way on the front porch.
- Jesus and I can walk around Franklin Park within forty-five minutes.
- Jesus and I can swing my arms back and forth without pain in my shoulders.
- Jesus and I can do weekly laundry.
- Jesus and I can vacuum my bedroom once a week.
- Jesus and I can make my bed every day.
- Jesus and I make breakfast every morning.
- Jesus and I make blueberry and corn muffins.
- Jesus and I made a pot of vegetable soup.
- Jesus and I made my family breakfast once.
- Jesus and I can wash and dry the dishes.

- Jesus and I did everything together.
- Jesus and I went out together. I would not go any place without inviting Jesus first.
- Jesus and I went to the store together. I asked Jesus please lead me to buy only what's good for my health.

I am encouraged. I try my best to practice putting Jesus first at all times in my life. Each day is a precious gift from my Father to me.

I perceived in my spirit from My Father, "I will get you safely through this day and all your days. You face nothing alone nothing! The best way to get through each day is step by step with me."

To God be the glory and power forever and ever. Amen.

Faith Nuggets of Wisdom

*F*aith is a noun. Faith is something we have.

> God hath dealt to every man the measure of faith. (Romans 12:3)
>
> (Increase the measure of our faith.)
>
> So then faith cometh by hearing, and hearing by the Word of God. (Romans 10: 17)

Faith is substance of things hoped for.
Faith is the evidence of things not seen.
Faith is a feeling of expectation.
Faith is having a desire for a certain thing to happen.

Faith is having a feeling of trust.

Faith is action.

Faith begins where the will of God is known.

Faith is a spiritual language of the heart.

Faith is the language God's children speak to him in words.

Faith is the conversation our God responds to.

The best way to act on the Word of God is to speak the Word. Decree and declare the Word of God.

Faith give God the privilege to work through us.

Faith results in a changed life and good works.

Faith involves a commitment of your whole self to God.

True faith evidenced by works.

> Even so faith, if it hath not works {action} is dead, being alone.
>
> Yea, a man may say, thou hast faith, and I have works: shew me thy faith without thy works, and I will shew thee my faith by my work. (James 2:17–18)

Faith says, "I know him. I believe! I obey!"

Trust is a verb. Trust is something we *do*. Praise God. Trust is faith in action. It is the manifestation of our *faith* in our thoughts and actions.

Faith says, "He is my healer."

> You were wounded for my trans-gressions, you was bruised for my iniquities; the chastisement for my peace was upon you, and by his stripes I am healed. (Isaiah 53:5)

> "For I will restore health unto thee, and I will heal thee of thy wounds," saith the Lord. (Jeremiah 30:17.)

The key to receiving healing in our minds and bodies is in the precious Word of God. First, we must confess with our mouth the Word of God. Second, then we can release our faith.

We must act on God's Word by confessing. So confessing plus acting (believing) is *faith*.

Now we are ready to receive our answer from our Heavenly Father.

Oh, bless God. His word is truth!

Present-time herbal intake:

- Garlic oil pearls, 500mg
- Cod liver oil, 1 tablespoon daily
- Ezzeac Plus or Cat's Claw, 2 tablespoons with
- Whole leaf aloe vera, 2 tablespoons in 4 oz. distilled water.
- Super vitamin C with Rose Hips, 1000mg
- Bifidophilus Flora Force, 1 capsule daily
- Vitamin E, 800mg
- Super Calcium, 1200mg
- Ionic minerals, 2 tablespoons daily
- Liquid Health complete multiple vitamin, 2 tablespoons daily
- Barley green, 1 tablespoon three times daily with a mixture of a variety of juiced different vegetables, 8oz three times daily.
- Proactazyme Plus, 1 capsule three times daily
- Super Omega-3 EPA, 2 capsules daily

I am the Lord that healeth thee.
(Exodus 15:26)

If we want God to care for us, we need to submit to his direction for living.

Health needs to be taught from a biblical perspective. God said that man would live 120 years (Genesis 6:3). Question! Why are we dying so young?

Could it be that we need to go back to the garden, the biblical perspective? "Beloved, I wish above all things that thou mayest prosper and be in health, even as thy soul prospereth" (3 John 2).

Could it be due to the deficiency of nutrients within our food that we eat and the toxicity that occurs from us eating those foods, our bodies have been incapable of receiving our healing God has instilled in our bodies!

God, our Creator, gave us guidelines for every aspect of our lives—how we should live to be healthy and how we should avoid disease. You know he did create our bodies to live forever. He placed within us capability for self-healing.

> And God said, 'Behold, I have given you every herb bearing seed, which is upon the face of all the earth, and every tree, in the which is the fruit of a tree yielding seed; to you it shall be for meat. (Genesis 1:29)

Yes, God gave us directions to what we should feed our bodies so that we might have total health. But after the fall, we do know that man would not live forever, but man still have within him the capability of maintaining health only if he would follow the guidelines that was given to him by God. Today, that same self-healing property remains within us. Thank you, Jesus. With every injury, our bodies attempt to accomplish that same task—self-healing—that was created within us. Thank you, Jesus, for such a miracle that was created in our bodies, with the built-in ability of self-healing without any external diagnosis.

We thank you, Father God, that our greatest *miracle* is not the healing of our bodies but the greatest miracle is the miracle of salvation, the forgiveness of our sins.

> For God so loved the world, that he gave his only begotten Son, that whosoever believeth in him should not perish, but have everlasting life. (John 3:16)

A Prayer for Health and Healing

Most Gracious Father, in the precious name of Jesus, I confess your word concerning health and healing. I truly believe that your word will not return to you void but it shall accomplish that which please you, and it shall prosper in the thing where you sent it.

In the name of Jesus, I do believe that I am healed according to Isaiah 53: 5 and 1 Peter 2:24. Your Word says that Jesus himself took my infirmities and bore my sickness. So with great boldness and confidence, I stand on the authority of your precious word, and I decree and declare that I am redeemed from the curse of sickness.

Satan, I serve you notice in the name of Jesus, I declare that your principalities, powers, rulers of the darkness of this world and spiritual wickedness in heavenly places are bound from operating against me in any way. I am loosened from your assignment. I am the property of Almighty God, and I give you no place in me, my life, nor my family life. I dwell in the secret place of the Most High God, and I abide under the shadow of the Almighty, whose power no foe can withstand. Father, I truly believe your Word that says, "The angel of the Lord encamps round about me and delivers me from every evil work. No evil shall befall me, no plague or calamity shall come near my dwell."

I confess that the Word abides in me, and it is life and medicine to my flesh.

The law of the Spirit of life in Christ Jesus operates in me, making me free from the law of sin and death.

I hold fast to my confession of your Word, and I stand immovable, knowing that health and healing are mine, in the precious name of Jesus.

Amen.

"Whose Report Shall
You Believe?"
Lyrics by Ron Kenoly

Whose report will you believe?
We shall believe
The report of the Lord

His report says
I am healed
His reports says
I am filled
His report says
I am free
His report says victory.

Behold, I am the Lord, the God
of all flesh: is there anything too
hard for me? (Jeremiah 32:27)

No! No! There is nothing too hard for our Lord God to do!

Father, in the name of Jesus, let every person who reads this book, let them be *highly favored*, *greatly blessed*, and *deeply loved* by you in the precious holy name of Jesus. Amen.

About the Author

I was the fourth child God loaned to my parents, Ms. Sallie L. and Mr. Rudolph Harley. I was born in Liberty County, Georgia, about forty-five minutes outside of Savanna. After I graduated from Liberty County High School, May 29, 1962, I moved to Boston, Massachusetts, to join my parents. Boston is where I met and married my husband. To our union, we were blessed with three loving children: Cheryl Ann, Erick Kelvin, and Donald Fredrick, and three more loving children, Audrey, Edward, and Nicole. I have ten grandchildren and one great-grandchild.

After being faithfully married for thirty-one years and nine months, God called my husband home September 16, 1993.

My education included the following: 1974 Boston Police Department Civilian Certificate School Traffic Supervision; 1976 Visiting Nurses' Association; 1980 N. E. Medical Hospital, Boston Massachusetts; and finally, 1986 American Business Institute, Boston, Massachusetts, certificate in Computer Operation.

My achievements included the following: 1987 Massachusetts Department of Social Services for MAPP Foster Parent; 1990–1995 Licensed Family Day Care Home; 1992 DARE Family Service, Inc.

My life always included being part of church ministries. June 19, 1982, my family and I Joined Grace Church of All Nations. October 25, 1982, I attended Beth Bible Institute. July 7, 2000, I participated in the Loe Church of Christ, the Bible Correspondence Course. October 30, 2005, I was certified duly consecrated and licensed as a minister. I was also a participant and completed the Grace Institute of Ministerial and Doctrinal Studies.

12/07/2019

To My Angel Greece

Trust God in the Storm
of Chaos,
Be Blessed!

Elder Albright-James

CPSIA information can be obtained
at www.ICGtesting.com
Printed in the USA
JSHW011628061119
2290JS00005B/32

9 781644 928004